DEPARTMENT OF THE NAVY
HEADQUARTERS UNITED STATES MARINE CORPS
2 NAVY ANNEX
WASHINGTON, DC 20380-1775

OPERATIONAL SUPPORT AIRLIFT MANAGEMENT

DEPARTMENT OF THE NAVY
HEADQUARTERS UNITED STATES MARINE CORPS
2 NAVY ANNEX
WASHINGTON, DC 20380-1775

MCO 4631.10A
ASM-4
29 Apr 97

MARINE CORPS ORDER 4631.10A

From: Commandant of the Marine Corps
To: Distribution List

Subj: OPERATIONAL SUPPORT AIRLIFT MANAGEMENT

Ref: (a) MCO 4630.21
      (b) DoDINST 4500.56
      (c) OPNAVINST 4631.2
      (d) Operational Support Airlift (OSA) Users Guide, 19 Sept 96
      (e) OPNAVINST 5410.13
      (f) DoDINST 4515.13 (NOTAL)
      (g) DoDINST 4500.9 (NOTAL)
      (h) MCO P4030.19F
      (i) Joint Federal Travel Regulations
      (j) MCO P4600.7C
      (k) MCO 4630.16B

Encl: (1) USMC Validating Activities
      (2) Standard Airlift Request Form MC11330
      (3) Validation and Authorization Procedures
      (4) VIP Codes

1. <u>Purpose</u>. This Order amplifies the policies of references
(a) through (k) and establishes the procedures for the peacetime
operation and management of Operational Support Aircraft (OSA).
This includes Marine Corps aircraft designated Operational
Support Airlift (OSA) as defined by reference (a) and other
logistics capable COMMARFOR aircraft when performing outside of
the scope of their primary assigned mission.

2. <u>Cancellation</u>. MCO 4631.10.

3. <u>Definitions</u>

   a. <u>Operational Support Airlift (OSA)</u>. Includes all airlift
transportation in support of command, installation or management
functions using DoD owned or controlled aircraft. Excludes
transportation provided through Airlift Service Fund (ASIF), support

of presidential, attache, and Security Assistance Organizations, and aircraft assigned to the 89th Military Airlift Wing.

b. <u>Operational Support Aircraft</u>. Those fixed-wing or rotary-wing aircraft acquired and/or retained exclusively for OSA, as well as any other DoD owned or controlled aircraft used for OSA purposes.

c. <u>Joint Operational Support Airlift Center (JOSAC)</u>. The joint scheduling activity assigned responsibility to schedule all valid CONUS OSA airlift requests and coordinate requirements with the requester and reporting custodian of OSA aircraft on all scheduled missions. JOSAC is located at the United States Transportation Command (USTRANSCOM), Scott AFB, IL.

d. <u>Joint Air Logistic Information System (JALIS)</u>. JALIS is the automated scheduling system utilized by all Services to provide validated airlift requests to JOSAC for action.

e. <u>Validating Activity</u>. The agency(ies) assigned responsibility to validate and input OSA airlift requests into JALIS to JOSAC for action.

f. <u>Field Validators</u>. Personnel assigned to validating activities who are tasked with the responsibility for receiving, processing, verifying passengers/cargo eligibility, assessing priority of travel, and inputting valid airlift requests into JALIS.

g. <u>Valid Request</u>. An airlift request which has been verified to contain all required approval authorizations and correctly prioritized using the Priority Urgency Justification Category (PUJC) codes.

h. <u>Aircraft Custodian</u>. Unit(s) assigned OSA aircraft as their Primary Aircraft Authorization (PAA).

4. <u>Background</u>

a. The DoD has established an inventory of OSA aircraft which is based solely on wartime requirements, and which operate in accordance with reference (a). Marine Corps OSA requirements have been established and are reviewed annually to ensure an appropriate level of OSA resources are maintained for wartime needs.

b. Reference (b) is the Secretary of Defense memorandum on the Use of Government Aircraft and Air Travel. This memorandum prescribes guidelines for the most effective use of airlift resources, and provides reporting and requesting procedures for the use of OSA assets. All DoD components are directed to comply with this memorandum.

    c. The fleet of Marine OSA consists of C-9B, UC-12, CT-39, and C-20 aircraft.

    d. On 10 October 1995, the Chairman of the Joint Chiefs of Staff (CJCS) tasked USTRANSCOM to evaluate CONUS OSA operations and provide recommendations to increase efficiencies. The Secretary of Defense accepted two USTRANSCOM recommendations forwarded by CJCS and tasked the Services with the following:

        (1) retain ownership of OSA aircraft; and

        (2) consolidate scheduling under USTRANSCOM management.

    e. USTRANSCOM established JOSAC to maximize use of available CONUS OSA assets to support the highest priority requests by optimally programming, planning, scheduling, modifying, executing and tracking CONUS OSA missions.

5. **Policy**

    a. DoD maintains and operates an inventory of DoD OSA aircraft to meet approved DoD emergency and wartime requirements with due regard for available commercial transportation. Marine Corps OSA and the associated operating and management structure will be maintained at a level that will ensure emergency and wartime requirements can be met. These aircraft will be used in peacetime to provide essential training for operational personnel, cost effective seasoning of pilots, and the transport of passengers and cargo where military needs dictate. When these aircraft perform wartime or emergency missions, cost effectiveness requirements outlined in this Order are not applicable.

    b. Marine Corps OSA aircraft are assigned to organizations or commands to satisfy valid transportation requirements in support of internal administration and management functions as outlined in Title 10 U.S.C. 5013(b). Requirements for OSA outside these functions are to be referred to the Air Mobility Command (AMC) in accordance with reference (e).

c. Operational readiness shall be achieved within approved flight hour programs.

d. JOSAC is the scheduling authority. The Marine Corps shall maintain validating activities to coordinate OSA airlift requests with JOSAC.

e. Headquarters Marine Corps (HQMC), Aviation Manpower and Support (ASM), Aviation Support Coordination Office (ASCO) shall act as the Marine Corps liaison with JOSAC. All concerns regarding JOSAC policy shall be directed to this office for action.

f. The priority of travel on military aircraft is to be determined on the basis of mission impact, rather than the rank of the requester. Scheduling and approving officials should follow the Airlift Priority System in reference (a).

g. Eligibility criteria for passenger traffic is established by reference (f).

h. Tactical (Fleet Marine Force organic) aircraft shall not be used for OSA missions except under extraordinary circumstances and with approval of the Deputy Chief of Staff for Aviation. Additionally, the tactical aircraft must have already been scheduled for an official purpose and the travel must:

(1) be on a noninterference basis;

(2) not require a larger aircraft than already scheduled for the mission;

(3) not require that scheduled official travelers or cargo be displaced; and

(4) result in negligible additional costs to the Government.

i. All OCONUS OSA airlift requests will be forwarded via message to CMC Washington DC//ASM// for action.

j. All Marine Corps band airlift requests will be forwarded via message to CMC Washington DC//ASM/PA// for action.

k. OSA shall not be requested if appropriate ground transportation can provide movement to required destination within a period not to exceed 60 minutes.

l. The uniform for passengers for all operational support airlift flights may be appropriate civilian attire or the uniform of the day as directed by the requesting unit.

m. Hazardous materials will be prepared and certified for air transportation in accordance with reference (g).

6. Responsibilities

a. The Air Support Coordination Office (ASCO), Aviation Department, HQMC, is the USMC liaison to JOSAC on all policy and scheduling issues. Additionally, this office is responsible for:

(1) advising CMC and DC/S Aviation on all matters pertaining to operational support airlift;

(2) ensuring effective airlift management and utilization of all Marine Corps operational support aircraft;

(3) ensuring implementation of JALIS within the Marine Corps in accordance with reference (d);

(4) reviewing this Order at the beginning of each calendar year, or as necessary, and submission of appropriate changes;

(5) consolidating quarterly flight hour messages and submit to JOSAC; and,

(6) preparation/submission of reports, as required.

b. Validating activities for OSA are the various Aviation Transportation Coordination Office (ATCO) sections at Headquarters Marine Corps; Commander, Marine Corps Air Bases, East (COMCABEAST); Commander, Marine Corps Air Bases, West (COMCABWEST); Marine Corps Air Station (MCAS) Futenma; and Commanding General, 4th Marine Aircraft Wing. These activities are responsible for:

(1) coordinating with the scheduling activity (JOSAC) on all OSA requests within the guidelines of references (a) through (k), with particular emphasis on use of the JALIS for scheduling and cost

comparisons as described in reference (d);

(2) providing airlift request status to the requesting agency 5 days prior to requested movement date; and

(3) entry into JALIS of all monthly Post Mission Reports (PMR), of the subordinate aircraft custodians, on the first workday following the flight, as outlined in reference (d).

c. In addition to the above general responsibilities, the following specific duties are assigned:

(1) HQMC ASCO shall:

(a) validate and process airlift requests (regardless of cost effectiveness) originating from within Headquarters Marine Corps; CG MCCDC, Quantico, VA; Marine Barracks, Washington, DC; and other DoD organizations in the Washington, D.C. area;

(b) refer approved OSA requests on tactical aircraft to the appropriate command; and

(c) schedule all USMC OCONUS OSA mission support.

(2) COMCABEAST ATCO shall:

(a) validate and process airlift requests (regardless of cost effectiveness) originating from COMMARFORLANT, the 2d Marine Aircraft Wing and Marine Corps Bases, Air Stations and independent Marine Corps activities located east of the Mississippi River (exclusive of the Washington, D.C. area);

(b) coordinate scheduling of Marine OSA aircraft located at MCAS Beaufort, MCAS Cherry Point, and MCAS New River with the scheduling activity (JOSAC); and,

(c) submit quarterly flight hours available for JOSAC scheduling to HQMC ASCO.

(3) COMCABWEST ATCO shall:

(a) validate and process airlift requests (regardless of cost effectiveness) originating from COMMARFORPAC, the 3d Marine Aircraft Wing, and Marine Corps Bases, Air Stations and independent Marine Corps activities located west of the Mississippi River;

(b) coordinate scheduling of Marine OSA aircraft located at MCAS El Toro and MCAS Yuma with the scheduling activity (JOSAC); and,

(c) submit quarterly flight hours available for JOSAC scheduling to HQMC ASCO.

(4) CO MCAS Futenma shall:

(a) validate and process airlift requests (regardless of cost effectiveness) originating from CG III MEF, 1st Marine Aircraft Wing and Marine Corps Bases, Air Stations and independent activities located in the western Pacific;

(b) schedule Marine OSA aircraft located at CO MCAS Futenma and CO MCAS Iwakuni.

(5) 4th Marine Aircraft Wing ATCO shall:

(a) validate and process airlift requests (regardless of cost effectiveness) originating from COMMARFORRES, 4th Marine Division, 4th Marine Air Wing, and 8th Marine Corps District;

(b) coordinate scheduling of Marine OSA aircraft located at NAS New Orleans with the scheduling activity (JOSAC); and,

(c) submit quarterly flight hours available for JOSAC scheduling to HQMC ASCO.

(6) Marine Corps Representative at NALO shall provide liaison with the authorized scheduling activity for passage of airlift requests to the DoN for OSA missions which cannot be satisfied with existing USMC assets.

(7) Marine Corps Representatives at JOSAC are responsible for:

(a) liaison with HQMC ASCO on all policy and scheduling issues that affect the management and utilization of USMC OSA aircraft.

(b) assisting CMC in submission of monthly reports to the SecDef on senior federal official travel; and,

(c) coordination of any special reports requested by the CMC (HQMC ASCO).

(8) <u>Aircraft Custodians of OSA Aircraft shall</u>:

(a) provide OSA aircraft as directed by JOSAC;

(b) implement a training program which will maintain sufficient aircrew in a ready status to meet emergency and wartime requirements, and all scheduled peacetime operations;

(c) provide, via JALIS, an aircraft status report of all forecasted non-available aircraft to the scheduling activity (JOSAC);

(d) ensure the preparation and submission of PMR's to JALIS the next working day following the completion of all flights (OSA, training, PMCF); and,

(e) submit quarterly flight hours available for JOSAC scheduling to the validating activity.

7. <u>Requests for OSA Transportation</u>

a. Supported units are responsible for submitting airlift requests via message as outlined in enclosure (2), or via NAVMC 11330, Request for Transportation form, enclosure (3). These requests will be forwarded to the appropriate Validating Activity listed in enclosure (2). CMC WASHINGTON DC//ASM4// shall be an info addressee on all airlift request messages.

b. Units are required to identify the purpose of travel in paragraph 9 of the airlift request message, or in the block titled "Specific Purpose of Travel", NAVMC 11330. This will allow the validating activity to ensure the appropriate priority and justification codes are assigned.

c. Airlift requests will be signed by the senior official traveler.

d. Supported units must ensure that all individuals listed on the request will be traveling on funded Government, or civilian invitational, travel orders in accordance with reference (i).

8. <u>Requests for Transportation of DoD Senior Officials, General/Flag Rank Officers</u>

a. Transportation requests for DoD senior officials and general/flag officers, other than Required Use and Official Duty Required Use travelers, as defined by reference (b), shall be submitted in writing to HQMC ASCO (CMC WASHINGTON DC//ASM4//) for validation. The request format is shown in enclosure (3).

b. The request will be signed by the senior official traveler certifying the need to use MilAir and to expend the associated costs. This signature authority may not be delegated.

c. <u>Funded Travel</u>. As outlined in reference (b), family member travel may be approved when there exists an unquestionably official function in which the family member will actually participate in an official capacity, or such travel is deemed in the national interest because of a diplomatic or public relations benefit to the United States. Submit family member travel requests to the Director, Marine Corps Staff (DMCS), for Assistant Commandant (ACMC) approval, info CMC WASHINGTON DC//ASM4//.

d. <u>Unfunded Travel</u>. Such travel is authorized for a family member only when accompanying a senior DoD official or other Federal official traveling on a military aircraft on official business. This category of travel differs from the space available privilege set forth in reference (f) in that it is limited to travel in the company of a senior DoD official and is reimbursable by the traveler at the full commercial coach class fare rate. Such travel is authorized on MilAir only under the following circumstances: (1) the aircraft is already scheduled for an official purpose; (2) this noninterference use does not require a larger aircraft than needed for the official purpose; (3) official travelers are not displaced; and, (4) it results in negligible cost to the government and the government is reimbursed at the full commercial coach class fare rate.

e. <u>Approval Authority</u>. COMMARFORLANT and COMMARFORPAC have blanket authority to have their spouses accompany them on official business when in the national interest. All other general officers will submit family member travel requests to CMC WASHINGTON DC//DMCS/ASM//.

9. <u>Validation and Authorization Process</u>

    a. OSA may be authorized when it is cost effective, or when it is required to accomplish the mission of the traveler considering any combination of the following factors:

        (1) travel destination,
        (2) itinerary,
        (3) schedule requirements,
        (4) security needs,
        (5) communications needs,
        (6) availability of commercial air, or
        (7) aircrew readiness training requirements.

The Deputy Chief of Staff for Aviation will authorize and validate travel for senior officials and general/flag officers.

    b. Validating activities will review, validate, and submit transportation requests in accordance with references (a) through (k).

    c. JALIS provides validating activities the ability to compute cost comparisons based on seat factors of the various OSA aircraft. Users may contact the validating activities for this comparison. References (c) and (d) contain detailed procedures for cost comparisons.

10. <u>Action</u>

    a. <u>CMC DC/S for Aviation (CMC (A)), Headquarters Marine Corps</u>. Maintain a Headquarters Air Transportation Coordination Office.

    b. <u>Headquarters Marine Corps ASCO</u>. Act as the Marine Corps liaison with JOSAC and Validating Activity for the National Capitol Region and, as such, coordinate the use of OSA in compliance with references (a) through (k).

    c. <u>Commanders, Marine Corps Air Bases, East and West, Commanding General, 4th Marine Aircraft Wing; Commanding Officer</u>, MCAS Futenma. Maintain air transportation coordination offices.

    d. <u>Operational Support Aircraft Reporting Custodians.</u> Shall provide:

(1) administrative, maintenance, and personnel support necessary to maintain and operate assigned assets;

(2) OSA aircraft to meet operational commitments; and,

(3) ensure the timely preparation and submission of PMR's in accordance with reference (d).

e. <u>Units Requesting Support</u>. Submit requests for operational support airlift missions in accordance with reference (d) and the instructions contained in enclosures (2) and (3).

11. <u>Records Disposition.</u> All flight requests, advisories, and communication pertaining to airlift shall be maintained for the current and 2 previous fiscal years at the validating activity which processed the airlift request.

R. I. NEAL
Assistant Commandant
of the Marine Corps

DISTRIBUTION: PCN 10206340600

Copy to: 7000110 (55)
7000093/8145005 (2)
7000099/8145001 (1)

USMC VALIDATING ACTIVITIES

1. The USMC validating activities have been established to provide regional support to OSA customers. All validating activities will coordinate support through JOSAC, USTRANSCOM.

2. Components of HQMC and Marine Corps activities within 50 nautical miles of Washington, DC, shall submit airlift requests to:

```
MSG:   CMC WASHINGTON DC//ASM4//
COMM:  (703)697-2411/241
DSN:   227-2411/2412
FAX:   227-2397
Mail:      Headquarters, U.S. Marine Corps
           (ASM-4 (ASCO))
           Washington, DC 20380-1775
```

3. Marine Corps activities east of the Mississippi River (exclusive of the Washington, DC area) shall submit airlift requests to the COMCABEAST ATCO, info CMC WASHINGTON DC//ASM4//.

```
MSG:   COMCABEAST CHERRY PT NC//SOPS//
COMM:  (919)466-4349/2838
DSN:   582-4349/2838
FAX:   EXT-4548
Mail:      COMCABEAST
           ATCO
           MCAS Cherry Point, NC 28533-5000
```

4. Marine Corps activities in CONUS west of the Mississippi River shall submit airlift requests to the COMCABWEST ATCO, info CMC WASHINGTON DC//ASM4//.

```
MSG:   COMCABWEST EL TORO CA//SOPS//
COMM:  (714) 726-3803
DSN:   997-3803
FAX:   997-4925
Mail:      COMCABWEST
           ATCO
           MCAS El Toro
           Santa Ana, CA 92709-5000
```

ENCLOSURE (1)

5. Marine Corps bases, air stations, and independent activities in the Western Pacific (WESTPAC) shall submit airlift requests to MCAS Futenma ATCO.

    ```
    MSG:  MCAS FUTENMA JA//ATCO//
    DSN:  (315)631-3064/3526
    FAX:  636-3759
    Mail:     Commanding Officer
              Attn: OPS Officer
              MCAS Futenma (Okinawa)
              FPO Seattle, WA 98772-5000
    ```

6. Components of MARFORRES Headquarters, 4th Marine Aircraft Wing, and 4th Marine Division are to submit airlift requests to 4th MAW ATCO, info CMC WASHINGTON DC//ASM4//.

    ```
    MSG:   FOURTH MAW//G3/ATCO//
    COMM:  (504)678-6564/1386
    DSN:   678-6564/1386
    FAX:   678-6563
    Mail:     Commanding General
              Attn: ATCO
              4th Marine Aircraft Wing
              4400 Dauphine Street
              New Orleans, LA 70146-5400
    ```

7. Marine representative to NALO:

    ```
    MSG:   NAVAIRLOGOFF NEW ORLEANS LA//MARREP//
    COMM:  (504)984-6393
    DSN:   363-6393
    FAX:   363-6393
    Mail:     Naval Air Logistics Office
              (Attn: Marine Representative)
              4400 Dauphine Street
              New Orleans, LA 70146-7500
    ```

ENCLOSURE (1)

<u>STANDARD AIRLIFT REQUEST FORM</u>

<u>General Instructions</u>. The AIRLIFT REQUEST message and Request for
Transportation fax sheet were designed to provide essential
information to the scheduling activity for input into JALIS. Use of
the standardized format prescribed for the Airlift Request message and
Request for Transportation form is essential. The message is the
preferred means of requesting airlift support; however, all senior DoD
officials/general officer travel requests must be sent using the
Request for Transportation form. Requesting activities must ensure all
entries are limited to the number of characters as shown in the sample
message formats (figure 1) and fax sheet (figure 2). To ensure proper
recognition of data to be entered into Centralized Army Aviation
Scheduling System (CAASS), the following general instructions are
mandatory and will be referenced in the detailed instructions as
applicable:

1. A COLON (:) is used to separate data names from data fields; a
slash (/) is used to separate data fields.

2. Time groups are 10 numeric characters in length, utilizing ZULU
time in the following order: day of month, 24 hour ZULU time, month,
year (e.g. 1300Z on 10 Nov 1992 would appear 1013001192).

3. The International Civil Aviation Organization (ICAO) location
identifier is the four-character code as found in enclosure (3) of
Department of Transportation Publication 7350.4p. Activities
requesting cod/vod services for a ship shall use the four-letter ship
call sign as it appears in enclosure (3) of ACP113(V).

4. Plain language origination and airfield names will be abbreviated
to a maximum of 10 characters. Use standard short titles as they
appear in the Plain Language Address Directory (NTP-3 Supp-1 (E)).
Delete\prefix titles such as NAS, MCAS, etc. For example, NAS North
Island would be represented by NORTH ISLA.

5. Dimensions are in inches and weight in pounds.

6. DO NOT "zero fill" or enter in unused data fields.

<u>Message Transmission</u>. The scheduling and/or coordinating activity
receives either a hard copy message or a fax sheet. If the

communication servicing center does not handle OCR messages, that center must be made aware that Airlift Request messages require special handling for both data and plain language transmission. Include in the Special Instructions section of DD 173 "Transmit line lengths as typed."

<u>Message Format</u>. The following paragraphs provide detailed nstructions designed to assist in preparing the Airlift Request. The paragraph numbers correspond to the numbers in brackets displayed in figure 1 to this enclosure.

1. <u>FROM</u>: Name of the command originating the message.

2. <u>TO</u>:   Name of the scheduling or coordinating activity receiving the Airlift Request.

3. <u>INFO</u>: Any command with a "need to know" about the Airlift Request. CMC WASHINGTON DC//ASM// must always be included as an INFO addressee.

4. <u>UNCLAS//N04631//</u>: This indicates that the Airlift Request message is unclassified and gives the correct subject code. If the mission is classified, the proper classification will be shown in lieu of "UNCLAS," however, all slashes should be omitted in the text, as this information will not be processed by the CAASS computer system.

5. <u>AIRLIFT REQUEST</u>: Must always appear as the subject line of the message.

6. <u>LIFT</u>:_____/ Each "leg" or portion of an airlift from one place to another is called a LIFT. Each Lift is designated in order by a letter, starting with "A" (e.g., LIFT:A/, LIFT:ZZ/) (maximum of two characters).

7. <u>Line 1 - Unit</u>:_____/ Name of the unit to which the personnel or cargo to be lifted are assigned (General Instructions 4).

8. <u>UIC</u>:_____/ Unit Identification Code for the unit to be airlifted. Unit identification codes may be found in chapter 5, volume 2, of the NAVSO P-1000-35, Rev. 39 (maximum of five numbers).

9. Line 2.A. - DEP ICAO:_____/ Enter the four-character ICAO for the airfield or call sign of the ship most expedient to the departure point for the lift (General Instructions 3).

10. PLACE:_____/ Plain language name of the airfield or ship identified by the DEP ICAO (General Instructions 4).

11. Line 2.B. - DESIRED:_____/ Most desirable departure time (General Instructions 2).

12. EARLIEST:_____/ Earliest travel availability time (General Instructions 2).

13. Line 3.A. - ARR ICAO:_____/ Four-character ICAO of the airfield or call sign of the ship most convenient for the arrival point of the lift (General Instructions 3).

14. PLACE:_____/ Plain language name of the airfield or ship identified by the ARR ICAO (General Instructions 4).

15. Line 3.B. - DESIRED:_____/ Most desirable arrival time (General Instructions 2).

16. REQUIRED:_____/ Arrival time which must be met to accomplish the mission (General Instructions 2).

17. Line 4. - PUJC:_____/ Priority, Urgency, Justification and Category codes for the requested airlift. Use the table in enclosure (5) to identify the appropriate codes (e.g., 22FZ; PRIORITY "2" for combat support; URGENCY "2" for operational; JUSTIFICATION "F" for fleet support; and CATEGORY "Z" for other than those listed) (maximum of four characters)).

18. Line 5. - PAX:_____/ Number of passengers to be airlifted.

19. BAG:_____/ Total weight, in pounds, of the baggage to be lifted with the passengers on this lift. Forty pounds of baggage are allowed per passenger (maximum of five characters).

20. Line 6.A - CARGO:_____/ Gross weight, in pounds, of the cargo involved. If only passengers and associated baggage are involved, omit lines 6.A-D.

21. <u>CARGO CUBE</u>: Overall volume of the cargo to be lifted, in cubic feet.

22. <u>TYPE CODE</u>: Type of cargo to be lifted according to cargo codes listed in enclosure (3). If more than one type of cargo is to be lifted, indicate the two most predominant types of cargo (maximum of two characters).

23. <u>Line 6.B. - LSI</u>:____/ Largest Single Item of cargo to be lifted. The LSI is described as inches length, inches, height, inches width, lbs. For example: "6.B. LSI:INL:31/INH:45/INW:45/LBS:92/. (Dimensions are a maximum of five characters) (General Instructions 5)).

24. <u>Line 6.C. - HSI</u>:____/ Identifies the Heaviest Single Item in the cargo to be lifted. (Utilize the same format as in item 23 above). For example, HSI: INL:92/INH:92/INW:52/LBS:5627/(General Instructions 5).

25. <u>Line 6.D.</u> - Plain language description of special handling required or description of cargo. (No limit on characters). This information is not scanned for entry into the Naval Air Logistics Information System.

26. <u>Line 7.A. - REQ COORD</u>:____/ Grade; name, autovon, FTS, or commercial phone number and location of the person to be contacted concerning any questions about the Airlift Request. If feasible, the "Request Coordinator" should be able to provide all required liaison for the requested air transportation (maximum of 34 characters).

27. <u>Line 7.B. - DEP COORD</u>:____/ If a separate departure coordinator (if the same as line 7.A., omit line 7.B.) (maximum of 34 characters)).

28. <u>Line 7.C. - ARR COORD</u>:   / If the same as "7.A." or "7.B." omit line "7.C." If a separate arrival coordinator is required, this line is to contain the identity of the Arrival Coordinator (maximum of 34 characters).

29. <u>Line 8. - VIP CODE</u>:____/ and <u>NAME</u>:____/ Senior official to be airlifted who is of the grade Marine Colonel/Navy Captain or senior. Type the last name of the VIP, and limit the name to eight characters.

ENCLOSURE (2)

VIP Codes are listed in enclosure (6). If no VIP is being lifted, omit line 8.

30. <u>Line 9. - REMARKS</u>. Special instructions and pertinent information concerning the requested airlift may be detailed in this line. It will include the purpose of the airlift and the reason commercial transportation was not used. This section has no character limit.

```
01  01  100005Z  NOV  92  PP     UUUU

FM      CG THIRD MAW//G3// (1)

TO      COMCABWEST EL TORO CA//SOPS// (2)

INFO    CMC WASHINGTON DC//ASM4// (3)

        MCAS EL TORO CA//BASEOPS//

        MCAS YUMA AZ//BASEOPS//

        NAVAIRLOGOFF NEW ORLEANS LA

UNCLAS  //N04631// (4)

SUBJ/AIRLIFT REQUEST// (5)

LIFT:A/  (6)

              (7)          (8)
1.  UNIT:CG THIRD MAW/UIC:M57081/
              (9)          (10)
2.A.  DEP ICAO:KNZJ/PLACE:EL TORO/
              (11)         (12)
2.B.  DESIRED:2116001192/EARLIEST:2115301192/
              (13)         (14)
3.A.  ARR ICAO:KNYL/PLACE:YUMA/
              (15)         (16)
3.B.  DESIRED:2117001192/REQUIRED:2118001192/

4.  PUJC:22AE/ (17)
     (18)   (19)
5.  PAX:6/BAG:240/
         (20)     (21)         (22)
6.A.  CARGO:200/CARGO CUBE:9/TYPE CODE:B/

6.B.  LSI INL:49/INH:42:INW:26/LBS:100/  (23)

6.C.  HSI INL:49/INH:42:INW:26/LBS:100/  (24)
```

FIGURE 1. SAMPLE AIRLIFT REQUEST.

0202   PP   UUUU

6.D. CARGO SPARE PARTS.   (25)

7.A. REQ COORD: MAJ WOODY AV 997-1234/   (26)

7.B. DEP COORD: MAJ HAYES AV 997-4321/   (27)

7.C. ARR COORD: CAPT GOODALL AV 951-9876/   (28)

8. VIP CODE:M7/NAME:JONES/   (29)

9. REMARKS. PURPOSE OF TRANSPORTATION TO INCLUDE ANY
AMPLIFYING REMARKS.//

NOTE: FOR TWO OR MORE LIFTS START REQUEST FORMAT AGAIN AND INDICATE
       WITH APPROPRIATE LIFT DESIGNATION, E.G., LIFT B, LIFT C, ETC.

FIGURE 1. SAMPLE AIRLIFT REQUEST-CONTINUED.

ENCLOSURE (2)

VALIDATION AND AUTHORIZATION PROCEDURES

1. <u>General Guidelines</u>. These procedures are provided as a guide to properly validate and determine required authorization for airlift requests. This order is designed to provide guidance for the majority of airlift requests but does not coverall possible situations.

   a. A valid request is a request which has been verified to contain all required approval authorizations and correctly prioritized using the Priority Urgency Justification Category (PUJC) codes.

   b. Only valid requests are entered into the Joint Air Logistics Information System (JALIS).

   c. The Deputy Chief of Staff for Aviation will authorize and validate travel for all senior officials and general/flag rank officials.

   d. Any airlift request not covered by these guidelines shall be directed to Headquarters Marine Corps (code ASM) for disposition.

2. <u>Submission and Receipt of Airlift Request</u>

   a. Requesters shall send airlift requests to the validating activity using the following methods:

      (1) Airlift request information provided via the U.S. Message Text Format as outlined in enclosure (2).

      (2) NAVMC 11330, Request for Government Air Transportation as outlined in enclosure (3).

   b. Marine Corps districts are to submit airlift requests for command visits directly to HQMC ASCO.

   c. Marine Corps band activities are to submit airlift requests for approved events to HQMC ASCO.

   d. Requests should be submitted as early as requirements are known. Group travel request of 8 or more passengers should be submitted at least 45 days in advance. All other requests should be submitted at least 7 days prior; however, all requests will be reviewed, and if determined to be valid, can be entered into the system regardless of lead time. The closer the request is submitted to the actual fly date, the less likely support would be provided.

e. All senior DoD officials and general/flag rank officer travelers must use the NAVMC 11330 request form in order to provide a written signature to the validating activity and thereby remaining in compliance with the DoD Memorandum, Use of Government Aircraft and Air Travel of 30 OCT 1995.

3. <u>Review and Validation of Airlift Request</u>. The field validator at the Validating Activity will review the request to ensure all information is complete and legible. The requester is responsible for any missing or incomplete information. In reviewing the request, the field validator will establish eligibility of the passengers/cargo and assign a valid Priority Urgency Justification Classification (PUJC) code.

  a. <u>Establish Passenger Eligibility</u>

    (1) DoDINST 4515.13, Air Transportation Eligibility will be used to establish the eligibility of passengers for the purposes of embarkation aboard government owned or controlled aircraft.

    (2) Comply with all requirements in DoD Memorandum, Use of Government Aircraft and Air Travel of 30 OCT 1995, for all airlift requests from DoD Senior Officials and General/Flag rank Officers.

    (3) Field validators shall process the following categories of passengers for embarkation aboard OSA aircraft as space required travelers without any additional written authorization from an approving authority:

      (a) Active duty military on official travel orders (TDY or TAD);

      (b) U.S. civilian DoD employees on official travel orders (TDY or TAD);

      (c) Reservist on official travel orders in conjunction with regular duties.

(4) Field validators shall obtain written authorization from either HQMC, COMMARFORPAC, COMMARFORLANT, COMMARFORRES, COMCABEAST, or COMCABWEST for the following categories of passengers for embarkation aboard OSA aircraft:

    (a) Foreign Nationals (military);

    (b) U.S. civilian employees of DoD contractors;

    (c) Local U.S. civilian news media representatives in terms of the scope of interest and as to the distance of travel involved.

(5) HQMC (ASM/ASCO) is the approval authority for all other categories of passengers to include, but not limited to the following:

    (a) Senior Federal Officials;,

    (b) General/Flag rank officers;

    (c) Non DoD Civilians;

    (d) Members of Congress and their staff;

    (e) Spouses of active duty military personnel;

    (f) Non-Local U.S. civilian news media representatives in terms of scope of interest and/or as to the distance of travel.

  b. <u>Establish Eligibility of Cargo</u>

(1) DoDINST 4515.13, Air Transportation Eligibility will be used to establish the eligibility of cargo for the purposes of embarkation aboard Government owned or controlled aircraft.

(2) MCO P4030.19F, Hazardous Material order shall be used to certify all hazardous material for flight.

(3) A waiver shall be obtained to transport restricted materials and passengers together.

(4) Field validators shall process the following categories of

cargo for movement on a space required basis without any additional written authorization from an approving authority:

    (a) DoD cargo;

    (b) U.S. military mail;

    (c) Defense Courier Service material;

    (d) Cargo of DoD contractors, if such transportation is specified in the contract.

    (5) HQMC (ASM/ASCO) is the approval authority for all other categories of cargo to include, but not limited to the following:

    (a) Cargo of other U.S. Government agencies;

    (b) Non-U.S. Government cargo;

    (c) Cargo in connection with special DoD programs.

    c. Assign Priority/Urgency/Justification/Category (PUJC) Codes. The field validator will assign PUJC codes based on the stated purpose of travel of the requester.

    (1) Passenger/Cargo Priority Codes. The first character shall be selected by the requester on the airlift request form; however, the field validator shall ensure the proper priority is actually entered in JALIS from one of the following three codes listed in order of precedence:

    (a) Priority 1. (Emergency) Airlift in direct support of operational forces engaged in combat, contingency or peacekeeping operations directed by the National Command Authorities or for emergency lifesaving purposes.

    (b) Priority 2. (Required) Required use airlift requirements with the compelling operational considerations making commercial transportation unacceptable. Mission cannot be satisfied by any other mode of travel.

    (c) Priority 3. (Cost Effective / Space Available) Official business airlift which is validated by JOSAC to be more cost effective than commercial air travel when supported by military aircraft or official business permitting space available travel on previously scheduled missions. This will comprise the majority of airlift requests and will be submitted regardless of cost effectiveness.

(2) <u>Passenger/Cargo Urgency Codes</u>. The urgency code is the second character of the PUJC code. These codes are designed to promote uniformity in urgency criteria, yet are intended to be sufficiently flexible to permit appropriate priority to be assigned in terms of the end use of the passengers and/or cargo to be airlifted. The following codes are listed in order of precedence:

(a) <u>Urgency 1</u>. (Combat) Airlift of personnel or material in direct support of, or alerted for support ofoperational forces engaged in general war or national contingency operations.

(b) <u>Urgency 2</u>. (Lifesaving or Operational) Airlift of personnel or material in direct support of airlift for lifesaving preparations or operations by deployed forces or forces preparing for mobilization.

(c) <u>Urgency 3</u>. (Humanitarian) Emergency airlift of personnel or material in support of authorized and urgent humanitarian purposes.

(d) <u>Urgency 4</u>. (Critical) Airlift of personnel or material which, while not fulfilling a higher urgency, would critically impact the outcome of unit requirements if not immediately supported exactly as requested.

(e) <u>Urgency 5</u>. (Priority) Airlift of personnel or material not fulfilling a higher urgency, but which would have a serious impact on the outcome of unit requirements if not fulfilled. Changes or consolidation with other request would not adversely affect the unit requirements.

(f) <u>Urgency 6</u>. (Routine) Airlift of personnel or cargo scheduled as part of an organization's routine requirements. Changes to or consolidation with other requests would not affect unit requirements. Also includes airlift of personnel or cargo qualified on a cost effective or space available basis, including authorized reserve component personnel traveling to or from active and inactive duty training.

   (3) <u>Justification Codes</u>. The justification code comprises the third alphabetic code of PUJC. It is used to identify the purpose of the lift request. Justification codes will be assigned and verified by the field validator.

A - Administrative
B - Civil Works
C - Recruiting/Retention
D - Medical Support
E - Emergencies
F - Fleet Support (General)
G - Special Weapons/Components Movement
H - Seabee Support
I - Special Warfare Support
J - Research
K - Morale/Displaced Homeport Visit/USO Tours/R&R
L - Coast Guard Support
M - ROTC
N - Reserves
0 - Joint Staff/OSD Staff Support
P - Training
Q - Material (Use Standard Cargo Codes in place of Category Codes when using this Justification Code)
R - Maintenance
S - Drug Enforcement/Task Force
T - Mobilization/Demobilization
U - CVAM Tasking
V-Y Unused
Z - Other Support (Remarks required)

   (4) <u>Category Codes</u>. The category codes comprise the fourth alphabetic code of the PUJC. They are necessary for historical data collection, and will answer the question "who" is being served by the Department of the Navy organic airlift.

A - Meetings/Conferences (Includes spouse travel)
B - Ceremonies
C - Goodwill/Foreign Dignitaries (Includes spouse)
D - Inspections/Investigations/Courts/Boards
E - Legislative Affairs/Public Affairs

ENCLOSURE (4)

F - Fleet Support (Deployed Unit at Sea)
G - Fleet Support (Deployed Unit Ashore)
H - Fleet Support (Ship Load out for Deployment)
I - Fleet Support (Ship Off load from Redeployment)
J - Unit Deployment/Redeployment (Other than Ship)
K - Fleet Support (Other)
L - Educators/Military Academies
M - Performer/Bands/Choirs/Drill Teams/etc.
N - Research and Development
O - DoD Contractors/Technicians Support
P - Consultations and Appointments(Med/Dent/Surgical)
Q - Marine Research
R - Wartime
S - Exercise
T - Unit Training (Active Units)
U - Unit Training (Reserve Components)
V - Test Flights
W - Readiness Training
X - Aviator Training
Y - Ferry Flight (Aircraft or Aircrew)
Z - Other
1 - Evacuation of Aircraft
2 - Evacuation of Personnel
3 - Aeromedical Evacuation (MEDEVAC)
4 - Other Evacuation
5 - Search and Rescue (SAR)
6 - Medical Support (Organ/Tissue/Blood Transfer)
7 - Graves Registration/Body Removal
8 - Emergency Ordnance Disposal (EOD)
9 - Disaster Relief/Other Crisis Relief

      (5) Type Cargo Codes. Select the appropriate cargo code from
the list below and ensure special handling instructions are entered in
the remarks section.

A - Mail
B - Aircraft Spares, Parts
C - Avionics Spares, Parts
D - Aircraft Engines
E - Electronic Parts
F - Test Equipment
G - Ground Support Equipment

L - POL Products (Ensure Packaging Requirements are met)
H - Video Equipment
I - Medical Equipment
J - Organizational Equipment
K - Maintenance Equipment/Tools
M - Explosives (Ensure Transportation Requirements are met)
N - Weapons (Ensure Transportation Requirements are met)
O - Weapons Systems Parts
P - Missiles (Ensure Transportation Requirements are met)
Q - Chemicals (Ensure Transportation Requirements are met)
R - Subsistence
S - Musical Instruments
T - Human Remains
U - Not Mission Capable - Supply (NMCS) items
V - Not Mission Capable - Maintenance (NMCS) items
W - Other Aviation Cargo
X - Other General Cargo
Y - Hazardous Cargo

 d. Determination of passenger/cargo eligibility and assignment of
the PUJC code establishes the validity of the airlift request. A
valid request is a request which has all required approval
authorizations and has a correct PUJC code assigned by the field
validator.

4. Entering Airlift Request in JALIS. Only valid requests shall be
entered into JALIS. Once a request is entered in JALIS, the customer
shall contact the validation activity for status and modifications.

5. Modifications, Regrets and Cancellations. Airlift requests
received telephonically (voice/fax) will be modified, canceled, or
regretted telephonically. Airlift requests received by message will
be modified, canceled, or regretted via message. Since the computer
will use the words "AIRLIFT REQUEST" to begin processing the request
information, it is necessary to alter the message title for changes to
the initial request.

 a. Modifications. Requesters shall contact the validating
activity for modifications to their original airlift requests. In
turn, the field validator shall input this modification into JALIS and
only JOSAC shall determine if the modification can be accommodated
without disrupting other priority missions.

(1) A change in the requirements of the lift should be identified by referring to the Airlift Request message Date-Time-Group, and identifying the alphabetic character of the lift involved, and the paragraph number. Use the same format for that paragraph as in an initial Airlift Request. Use the words "MODIFICATION TO AIRLIFT REQUEST" as the subject line.

   b. Regrets. Regrets to Airlift Requests are made by the scheduling activity. JOSAC will notify both the requesting unit and the Validating Activity of the regret. A regret code will be assigned to the airlift request.

      (1) Regret Codes.

         A - No funds for OSA airlift (includes flight hours)
         C - Crew not available
         D - Duplicate request
         E - Commercial air more appropriate
         G - Ground/Helicopter transportation more appropriate
         H - Load/Requirement incompatible with available assets
         I - Immediate aircraft maintenance required
         L - Aircraft not available
         M - Weather
         N - Not cost effective
         R - Lifts reassigned to new mission
         U - Preempted by higher priority
         Z - Other

   c. Cancellations. A cancellation of an Airlift Request by the requester should refer to the Airlift Request message Date-Time-Group, and identify the alphabetic character of the lift or lifts involved. Use the words "CANCELLATION OF AIRLIFT REQUEST" as the subject line, and indicate a cancellation code. Those airlift requests received via NAVMC 11330 should be canceled telephonically with the Validating Activity.

      (1) Cancellation Codes.

         B - Unnecessary requirement
         F - Ground/Helicopter transportation more appropriate
         T - Canceled by requester
         Q - Original requirements changed

   d. <u>Short Fused Request and Modifications</u>. The field validator
shall contact JOSAC telephonically to determine if the short fused
request or modification can be accommodated.

<u>VIP CODES</u>

1. Data fields on JALIS documents requiring VIP codes should be filled by appropriate alpha-numeric combination from the following table. "NA" will indicate that no appropriate code applies. <u>Do not zero fill</u>.

    a. <u>Service/Agency/Affiliation</u>

       A - Air Force
       C - Coast Guard
       F - Foreign
       M - Marine
       R - Army
       S - Civilian
       V - Navy
       Z - Executive Service

    b. <u>Rank</u>

       1 - President, Heads of State
       2 - Vice-President, Cabinet Members, Members of Congress, CNO, CMC, Chief of Staff (other services), 5-star rank
       3 - Under Secretaries of Army, Navy, Air Force: 4-star rank
       4 - Lieutenant Generals (3-star), Vice Admirals, SES-5/6, GS-18 civilians, Assistant Secretaries in DoD
       5 - Major Generals (2-star), Rear Admirals Upper Half, SES-3/4, GS-17, Deputy Assistant Secretaries in DoD
       6 - Brigadier Generals (1-star), Rear Admirals Lower Half, SES-1/2, GS-16 civilians
       7 - Colonels, Captains (USN, USCG), GS-15 civilians
       8 - Senior Enlisted Advisors of the Armed Services

ENCLOSURE (5)